Need to Know
Sickle Cell
Disorder

Oliver Gillie

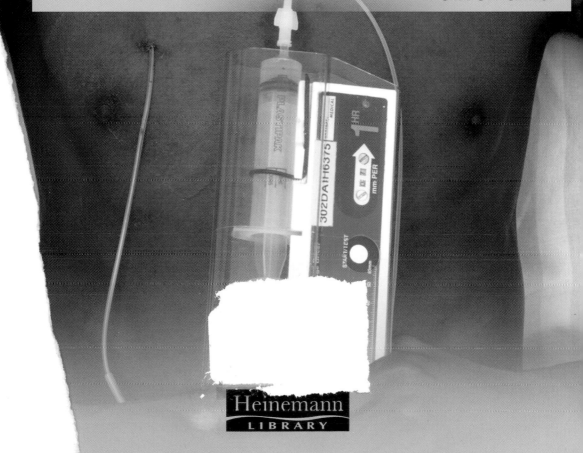

Heinemann
LIBRARY

www.heinemann.co.uk/library
Visit our website to find out more information about **Heinemann Library** books.

To order:
 Phone 44 (0) 1865 888066
 Send a fax to 44 (0) 1865 314091
 Visit the Heinemann Bookshop at www.heinemann.co.uk/library to browse our catalogue and order online.

Produced by Monkey Puzzle Media Ltd
Gissing's Farm, Fressingfield, Suffolk IP21 5SH, UK

First published in Great Britain by Heinemann Library, Halley Court, Jordan Hill, Oxford OX2 8EJ, part of Harcourt Education.
Heinemann is a registered trademark of Harcourt Education Ltd.

Editorial: Cath Senker
Design: Jamie Asher
Picture Research: Sally Cole
Production: Viv Hichens

Originated by Ambassador Litho Ltd
Printed and bound in Hong Kong, China by
  South China Printing Company

ISBN 0 431 09765 8
08 07 06 05 04
10 9 8 7 6 5 4 3 2 1

The publishers would like to acknowledge Marvelle Brown, Macmillan lecturer on sickle cell disorder at Thames Valley University, for her help in the preparation of the text.

British Library Cataloguing in Publication Data
Gillie, Oliver
Sickle Cell Disorder – (Need to know)
616.1'527
A full catalogue record for this book is available from the British Library.

Acknowledgements
The publishers would like to thank the following for permission to reproduce photographs: Alamy pp. 13 (Nicole Katano), 31 (Ami Vitale); Getty Images pp. 22 (Taxi), 26 (Image Bank), 39 (Taxi), 51 (Taxi); Hulton Archive pp. 6, 9; Panos pp. 28 (Mark Henley), 34 (Neil Cooper); Photofusion p. 11 (Crispin Hughes); Press Association p. 36 (Anthony Harvey); Science Photo Library pp. 1 (Alex Bartel), 5 (Eye of Science), 10 (Simon Fraser/RVI, Newcastle-upon-Tyne), 17 (Mark Clarke), 18 (Saturn Stills), 19 (Sue Ford), 21 (Ken Eward), 24 (BSIP/Laurent), 25 (St Bartholomews Hospital), 30 (Dr Gopal Murti), 32 (Alex Bartel), 42 (Alex Bartel), 43 (Sue Ford), 44–45 (Alex Bartel), 47 (Dr Rob Stepney), 49 (J. C. Revy); Topham pp. 4, 27, 40; Wellcome Photo Library pp. 14–15, 16–17, 33. Artwork on p. 23 by Michael Posen.

Cover photographs reproduced courtesy of Alamy/Dennis Kunkel/Phototake Inc. and Alamy/Yoav Levy/Phototake Inc.

The author would like to acknowledge the dedicated work of scientists and doctors who have advanced knowledge of sickle cell disorder and the important contribution of self-help groups that provide advice and help to those in need. Without these devoted people this book could not have been written.

Contents

Any words appearing in the text in bold, **like this**, are explained in the Glossary.

Introducing sickle cell disorder

'It is unbearable. Some people who have it just want to stop living. That's how bad it is. Nothing helps the pain,' says William Bratton, describing how he felt during an episode of sickle cell illness.

A fullback in an American football team at the University of Toledo in Ohio, USA, Bratton can normally lift 168 kilos in a bench press. That's about the weight of two adults! But after an episode of sickle cell illness he could barely lift 90 kilos. Playing football for his college is a struggle but he is an inspiration to his teammates.

'I get tired quicker than others – I'm gasping for air. I'm so tired I can't even drink water. It takes me two or three minutes before I have enough strength to go back out there,' says William.

People who have sickle cell disorder often suffer from painful attacks, which are called **crises**. During these crises they have pains in the arms, legs, back and stomach which may be very severe. Their hands and feet may swell, their joints become stiff and they feel extremely tired.

Hard exercise may bring on an attack of sickle cell disorder.

An inherited disorder

Sickle cell disorder is inherited. Its name comes from the red cells in the blood of sufferers, which take on the shape of a sickle (the crescent-shaped tool used when grain is harvested by hand). Sometimes it is called sickle cell disease because people who suffer from it can become very ill. And sometimes it is called sickle cell **anaemia** because they also generally become anaemic. That is, they have a reduced level of **haemoglobin**, the red-coloured substance in blood that contains iron and carries oxygen. Haemoglobin combines with oxygen in the lungs and then carries the oxygen all round the body.

Sickle cells

People who suffer from sickle cell disorder have a different type of haemoglobin from others. In people with the disorder, haemoglobin sticks together to form long rods inside red blood cells when the oxygen supply is low. This makes the cells rigid and then they often become sickle-shaped. As these sickle cells circulate in the blood they tend to get stuck in small blood vessels, cutting off the normal supply of oxygen and blood. This causes painful irritation and swelling, while the shortage of oxygen causes great tiredness.

Red blood cells from a person with sickle cell disorder. The normal cells are round, while some are sickle shaped.

History of discovery

In 1910 James B. Herrick, a doctor from Chicago, USA, put some blood from a West Indian patient under his microscope and looked at the red cells. Among the normal round-shaped red cells he saw a 'large number of thin, elongated, sickle-shaped and crescent-shaped forms,' as he later told the 25th annual meeting of the Association of American Physicians (doctors).

Dr Herrick was the first person to recognize sickle cell disorder but he was not sure what it was. The patient, Walter Clement Noel, was suffering from **anaemia**, a disease caused by a shortage of **haemoglobin**, the red-coloured substance in blood. But Dr Herrick was not sure whether the anaemia from which his patient was suffering was different from other types of anaemia.

Some 30 years after James Herrick discovered sickle cells, Linus Pauling (pictured here) showed that the haemoglobin of people with sickle cell disorder is chemically different from the haemoglobin of other people.

The first known victim of sickle cell disorder

Walter Clement Noel came from a wealthy family that owned the Duquesne Estate in the north of Grenada in the Caribbean. He went to study at the Chicago College of Dental Surgery in October 1904. As the northern winter brought the first cold weather, he came down with a chest infection. He was admitted to the Presbyterian Hospital where a doctor checked his blood cells and found that they were sickle shaped.

Walter Noel graduated in May 1907 and returned to Grenada where he set up a dental practice in the capital, St George's. Despite the sunny climate, Walter's chest problems returned and he died on 2 May 1916, aged 32.

Walter's case was later written up by Dr James B. Herrick. Walter became the first known victim of sickle cell disorder. If he had been a student in Chicago today he could have expected to live twice as long.

A new disease

Five years later two doctors at Washington University found another man with similar symptoms. They realized that they were looking at a new disease. Like the first patient the man was anaemic. And like him he had African ancestors, a yellowish tinge to the whites of his eyes and **ulcers** on his legs. These became the classic symptoms of sickle cell disorder.

In 1922 Verne Mason, a doctor at Johns Hopkins Hospital, Baltimore, in Maryland, USA, called the condition 'sickle cell anaemia' for the first time. The name stuck. A few years later John Huck, who had trained at Johns Hopkins Hospital, recognized that the disease was inherited according to the laws of **genetics**.

But it was not until 1949 that the way in which sickle cell anaemia can be inherited was fully understood. James V. Neel, working at the University of Michigan, was then able to explain why some people had only mild symptoms of the condition. These people are **carriers**. They can pass the condition on to their children but do not suffer from serious symptoms themselves.

Prejudice

Many of the scientists and doctors who carried out the early research into sickle cell disorder in the first half of the 20th century held racial **prejudices** that were common at that time.

In the early part of the 20th century many black people in the United States used to die from tuberculosis, a very infectious disease that spreads easily when people live in overcrowded conditions. Tuberculosis was much more common in the black than in the white population. Some people blamed a hereditary weakness of the 'black race'. Others disagreed and pointed to the poor living conditions of black people as the real cause.

Sickle cell disorder, then called sickle cell disease, was generally seen as a 'black' disease. It was quoted to support ideas that people of African descent were less healthy than whites. These ideas were used to help justify the racist argument that white people were superior to black people.

Sickle cell in whites

Some white people in Europe and North America suffer from sickle cell disorder. In the past, at a time when racial **discrimination** of all kinds was practised openly, this sometimes led to their race being questioned. Or, if there was no doubt about their race, then doctors questioned the diagnosis. They found it difficult to believe that a person with European ancestors could suffer from the disease. White people who carry the sickle cell **gene** most probably had ancestors who came from Africa. These ancestors may have been brought to southern Europe by the slave trade in ancient times. However, it is also possible that the gene originally came from more than one place.

In 1929 two American doctors reported several cases of sickle cell disorder in a Greek-American family of people described as 'racially pure whites'. They stated that the family came from 'Byregos, a small village in the Peloponnisos near Olympia where their families had long been residents and where negroes are said to be unknown'.

If Greeks could suffer from sickle cell disorder then the disease was not limited to black people alone. This went against the racist argument that black people were naturally less healthy.

Overcrowded living conditions in countries like the USA caused the spread of diseases such as tuberculosis among black people during the early 20th century.

One disorder among many

Individuals who suffer from chronic illness are often discriminated against. People at school or work may have no idea what they are going through. Some people may believe that it is a person's own fault that he or she is ill. Others just like picking on someone who they see as different.

To suffer from sickle cell disorder and to be of African descent brings the possibility of double **discrimination**. If it is suggested that the illness is a result of 'racial weakness', that makes the discrimination even worse. Science no longer recognizes any such thing. All groups of people suffer from certain inherited disorders that are more common among them than in others.

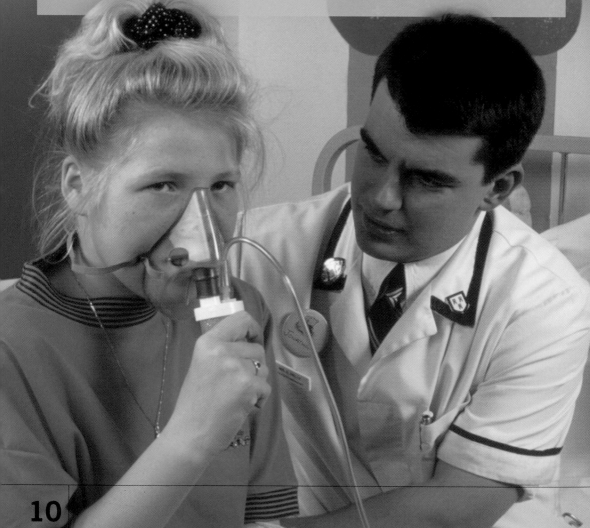

Inherited diseases

- Cystic fibrosis is an inherited disease that is much more common in people of European descent and relatively rare in people of African, Asian or Jewish descent. About 1 in 2500 babies with European ancestors inherit two **genes** for cystic fibrosis and develop the disease. They used to die in childhood from repeated lung infections. Nowadays with the help of **antibiotic** drugs they are able to live into adulthood. Even so they are repeatedly ill and the condition often stunts their growth and reduces the length of their life.

- Tay-Sachs disease is a hundred times more common among Ashkenazi Jews (Jews of eastern European origin) than in other groups of people. About 1 in 2500 Ashkenazi babies suffer from it. Children who are affected first show signs of the disease after about six months of age. They suffer from blindness, paralysis, **seizures** and other mental disturbances. They usually die before they are four.

- Phenylketonuria is a relatively common inherited disease in people with European ancestors but rare among people with African or Ashkenazi Jewish ancestors. If the disease is not diagnosed in the first few months of life, brain damage occurs. Fortunately it can be detected by a simple test and treated by diet. Then the child will develop normally.

- Porphyria is commonest among people of Scandinavian, Anglo-Saxon and German ancestry and rare in people with African ancestors. It causes distressing attacks of pain in the abdomen and can stop the nervous system from working, leading to death. It affected Britain's King George IV (1762–1830) and other members of European royal families.

This girl with cystic fibrosis is having treatment for lung disease.

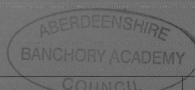

What is sickle cell disorder?

Sickle cell disorder affects many parts of the body. The irregular shape of the red blood cells prevents them from moving as freely through the blood vessels as normal red blood cells. They can cause blockages when they get stuck. This means sickle cells cannot carry oxygen around the body properly. Shortage of oxygen leads to damage, which is most severe in the smallest blood vessels. The damage can occur in almost any organ of the body, including the brain.

Bed rest can often provide relief from pain for people with sickle cell disorder.

Pain

The disorder causes extremely painful symptoms. Pain is most common in the arms, legs, back and stomach. The joints may also become stiff and painful. Boys may suffer from a stiff, painful penis, a condition called **priapism**. It sometimes starts as a pain in the groin. The condition is embarrassing for them and they may not want to mention it. But it is important to seek medical help. If it is not treated, damage may occur in the penis which leads to impotence (insufficient erection of the penis) later on in life.

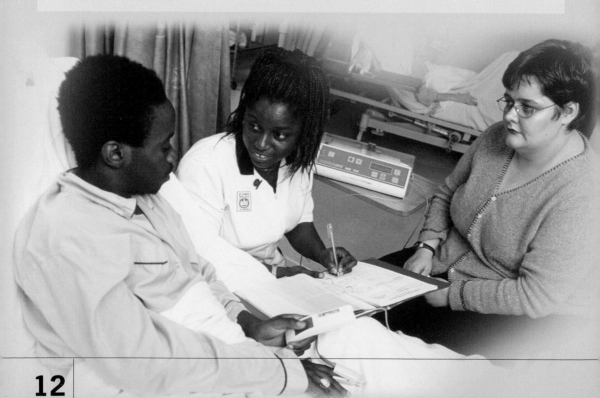

People with the disorder go through good and bad patches. Most people with the disorder suffer pain frequently. The pain often lasts all day and is associated about half the time with a feeling of great tiredness. Children with the disorder spend a lot of time in bed because rest brings some relief from exhaustion and pain.

Triggers for pain

Overexertion, overexcitement, cold weather, cold drinks and swimming have been found by many people to trigger pains. Bumps and bruises causing damage to **tissues** may also trigger an attack. One parent noticed that his daughter had an attack after taking a cold drink straight from the fridge. She has had less pain since drinks were served at room temperature. People with sickle cell disorder should drink frequently to avoid becoming **dehydrated**.

Sickle cell disorder is a serious condition but it is not like other more serious diseases that sometimes cause rapid death. For example, it is not the same as cancer, in which cells in a part of the body grow out of control and form a tumour. Nor is sickle cell disorder ever infectious.

Drinks served at room temperature are less likely to trigger pain among people with sickle cell disorder.

❝Finally I found out how to head off a crisis. I could feel the pain begin in my chest and back, and as it subsided in those areas the pain would travel into my arms, hips or legs, or all over my body. I now control my pain with oral Demerol tablets and oxygen, and lots and lots of fluids. ❞

(Inez Hardin, Sickle Cell Information Center, Emory University, Atlanta, Georgia, USA)

13

What is sickle cell disorder?

Effects on growth

Sickle cell disorder affects children's growth. Babies with sickle cell disorder are born at the normal size and weight and rarely show any symptoms of the disorder until after six months of age. But by the end of their first year or early in their second year they begin to grow more slowly. They continue to grow slower than normal. As adults they may be shorter and lighter than average. Growth of bones may be as much as five years behind normal, but people with sickle cell disorder do eventually catch up.

The increase in weight of children with the disorder is generally slower than the increase in their height. So they tend to be slim, if not thin. Men with the disorder tend to catch up in height by the age of 22 and women may actually be of above average height. Both men and women with the disorder tend to have long, thin arms and legs, and a relatively small body, narrow hips and shoulders.

Slower development

Men and women who suffer from sickle cell disorder are often slow to reach sexual maturity. Girls who have the disorder may have their first period later than others – on average at age 14 or 15 rather than at 12 or 13. The age when they have their first sexual experience and their first pregnancy also tends to be later. This is probably because slower physical development means that interest in sex is delayed.

Boys with the disorder are also slower to develop sexually. They have relatively low levels of the male **hormone testosterone** in their blood. They develop hair in their armpits, in the pubic area and on their faces later, and may be less **fertile**.

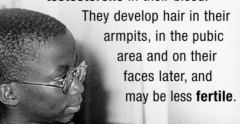

Pregnancy

Women with the disorder do not seem to be any less fertile than others. But pregnancy is likely to be more difficult. The risk of losing a baby is greater than normal. Women with sickle cell disorder should seek medical advice early in pregnancy. Where possible they should plan to have first-class care available even before starting a pregnancy. Regular check-ups during pregnancy will do much to reduce risks and bring the chance of a successful birth close to normal.

"As a child I longed to be normal. Now at seventeen I understand it is something that I might never obtain... Life for me has been hard. I was always ashamed of who I was. I know for a fact that I am not normal compared to teens of my age. I have been hospitalized over 100 times. As a child I was afraid to tell the truth about who I really am but now I let people know because I realize that this is part of me."

(Heidy Dodard, Sickle Cell Information Center, Emory University, Atlanta, Georgia, USA)

Young people with sickle cell disorder, such as the boy on the left, tend to have narrow hips and shoulders.

Sickle cell crises

People who suffer from sickle cell disorder have **crises** when the oxygen in their blood falls below 40 per cent of the normal level. During these crises they suffer severe pains in their muscles, bones and joints, as well as headaches, stiffness of the neck and shortness of breath. They also have **jaundice**, a yellowing of the whites of the eyes, which is more obvious than usual. The jaundice is caused by the destruction of sickle cells, which get broken down more quickly than normal red blood cells. This leads to the production of yellow-coloured substances from **haemoglobin** that circulate in the blood and can be seen in the whites of the eyes.

Sickle cell crises may happen to a person with the disorder at any time. These episodes of pain may be triggered by a mild infection such as a cold or flu, which cannot be predicted. A **virus** infection called parvovirus B19 often triggers crises. This virus circulates in the general population without causing serious illness, but people with sickle cell disorder are vulnerable to it.

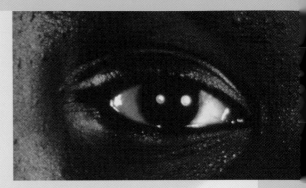

Yellow eyes are a sign of jaundice. Yellow-coloured substances are formed in the body when haemoglobin from damaged cells is broken down.

Hospital treatment

When a severe crisis occurs, urgent hospital treatment is required. Generally a person having a crisis is drowsy and cannot make decisions. Someone else may have to arrange to take the person to hospital.

In hospital the patient will be given pain relief. Fluids will be introduced into the body intravenously (through a vein) to correct and prevent dehydration. **Antibiotic** drugs will be given to prevent infection. Oxygen treatment will be given if the patient has a painful chest, which indicates that blockages are occurring in the small blood vessels of the lungs.

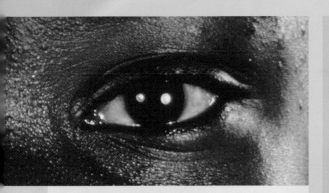

Some or all of these signs may occur in a sickle cell crisis:

- unusually severe pains in the abdomen, spine or chest
- headache
- stiffness of the neck
- fever
- drowsiness
- dark or red urine
- signs of possible damage to the nervous system, e.g. mental confusion or slurred speech.

Understanding the disease

Michael Cobb grew up in Asheville, North Carolina, USA, and as a kid he always did everything that other children did. He had a lot of crises but he wanted to prove that he could rise above them and so he joined the army aged 18.

'In my fifth week of boot camp I ran a mile and a half and went into a crisis. I felt once again my body giving way and not letting me do what I wanted to do,' explained Michael.

He ended up in the depths of despair. 'I was told I would not live to see the age of 35. I stopped caring about anything and everything. This led to more problems than you could ever imagine, drinking and taking drugs for about 10 years.'

Then he started to read about sickle cell disorder. 'Now at 37 I see that I could have done a lot more with my life. I never realized where I was going until I found out where I came from. It's all from the power of information.'

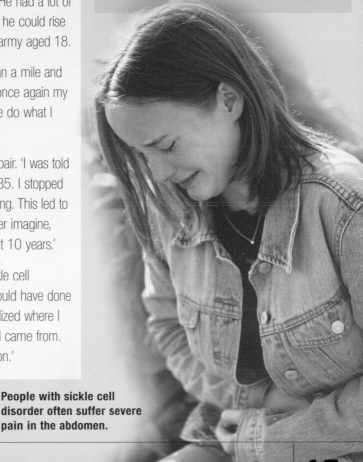

People with sickle cell disorder often suffer severe pain in the abdomen.

What is sickle cell disorder?

Symptoms

The first symptoms of sickle cell disorder may appear in infants at the age of about six months. At about this age babies may develop fever and swollen fingers. Called **dactylitis**, or hand-foot syndrome, it is very painful. The swelling and pain usually disappear within a week but appear again from time to time up to age three. This may result in damage to the small bones of the hands and feet. It can lead to poor control of finger movements later in life.

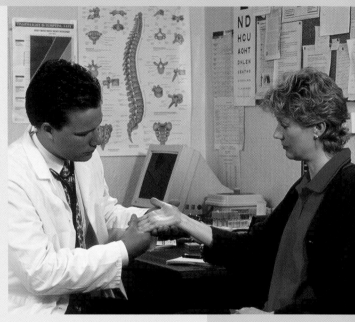

A doctor checks for anaemia, which is common in people with sickle cell disorder.

The spleen

Damaged red cells are removed from the blood by an organ in the abdomen called the **spleen**, which then recycles the haemoglobin. In children with sickle cell disorder the spleen has to work overtime and sometimes becomes choked with red cells. Very severe **anaemia** may then follow.

From an early age, the spleen of people with sickle cell disorder is unable to produce antibodies, the substances in the blood that protect against **bacteria** and viruses. This leaves children with the disorder open to serious infections, particularly **septicaemia** (blood-poisoning), which is caused by bacteria called pneumococci. The overworked spleen usually shrivels up and by adulthood no longer functions at all.

Bones and organs

Later in life the disorder may cause damage to growing bones, especially the backbone and the hip joint. This occurs because small blood vessels in the growing ends of bones become blocked by damaged sickle cells. The damaged cells cut off the oxygen supply that is essential for living tissue.

Similar damage may occur in the kidneys, the liver, the bowel and the lungs, causing severe breathing difficulty and sometimes **pneumonia**. People with the disorder often suffer from leg **ulcers**, caused again by the poor blood supply. And they may suffer **seizures** or a **stroke** when the brain is affected.

In Africa few people with the disorder live beyond the age of five, but in Jamaica (where good health services for sickle cell disorder have been pioneered) and in countries with a modern health service, most live on into their 50s or even 60s.

❝When I was in the 5th grade I ran a mile instead of telling my instructor that I was tired. I pushed myself and as a result missed the rest of the school year. In my Junior Year in College I was so stressed out about a test that I ended up in the emergency room due to a sickle cell crisis.❞

(Melissa Creary, Sickle Cell Information Center, Emory University, Atlanta, Georgia, USA)

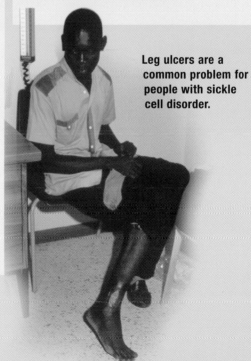

Leg ulcers are a common problem for people with sickle cell disorder.

Haemoglobin

The difference between a person with sickle cell disorder and a person without the condition is entirely due to a small difference in the make-up of their **haemoglobin**, the red substance in blood. Haemoglobin has a complicated structure that it has taken scientists many years to understand. They have found many different types of haemoglobin. Haemoglobin from people with sickle cell disorder is called haemoglobin S.

Haemoglobin is made up of **haem** (which contains iron), the part that combines with oxygen, and four **globin molecules**. Working together, the haem plus the four globins carry oxygen round the body from the lungs to other parts where the oxygen is used up. The difference between people with sickle cell disorder and others lies in the globin part of the haemoglobin molecule.

The structure of globin

Globin is a **protein** and, like all proteins, it is made up of hundreds of **amino acids** joined together like links on a chain. The amino acids in any particular type of protein are arranged in a particular order along the chain, giving that protein its own special character. Globin from people with sickle cell disorder differs from normal globin by just one of these amino acids in one position in the chain. The order of the amino acids in globin, and all other proteins in the body, is decided by the **genes** a person inherits.

This is a molecular graphic of the haemoglobin molecule. The haem group has been highlighted in colour.

Inheritance of sickle cell disorder

Sickle cell disorder is inherited. A person suffering from the disorder possesses two **genes** for **haemoglobin** S, one that has come from the father and one that has come from the mother. **Carriers** inherit only one gene for haemoglobin S and one for normal haemoglobin. They generally show few signs of the disease and remain in normal health throughout life.

The genes for haemoglobin behave exactly as predicted by Mendel's laws of inheritance. These were worked out by Gregor Mendel, an Austrian monk, in the 1860s. A child must inherit one haemoglobin gene from each parent, but otherwise it is a matter of chance which haemoglobin genes a child will inherit.

How Mendel's laws work

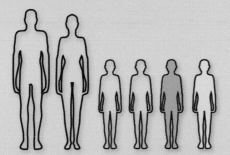

- When both parents are carriers there is a one in four chance that a child will suffer from sickle cell disorder. There is one chance in two that a child will be a carrier, and one chance in four that a child will neither have the disease nor be a carrier.

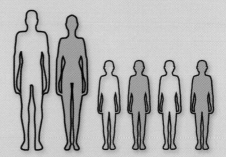

- If one parent has sickle cell disorder and another is a carrier there is a one in two chance that a child will be a carrier. The chance that a child will have the disorder is also one in two.

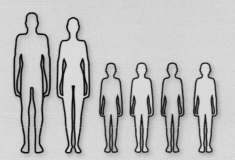

- If one parent is a carrier and the other is completely normal (neither a carrier nor suffering from the disorder) there is a one in two chance that a child will be a carrier. There is a one in two chance that a child will be normal.

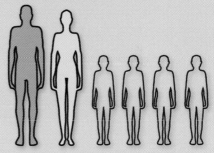

- If one parent has sickle cell disorder and the other is completely normal (does not have the disorder and is not a carrier) then all the children will be carriers.

☐ Carrier
☐ Normal
☐ Sickle cell disorder

Tests for the disorder

The basic test for sickle cell disorder can easily be done in any medical laboratory. A sample of blood is mixed with a special chemical on a glass slide and sealed with wax. The slide is left for 24 hours so that all the oxygen in the blood is used up by the chemical. If the person has the disorder, their red cells then change into the sickle form and can be seen clearly under a microscope.

However, this test cannot show the difference between people who have the disorder and people who are **carriers**. Their blood looks the same under the microscope. And the test does not work for babies because babies only have a small amount of sickle cell **haemoglobin** in their blood. For this reason, an electrophoresis test is generally preferred for diagnosis. In this test, an electric current is used to separate out the different types of haemoglobin. It enables carriers, babies with the disorder, and other types of abnormal haemoglobin to be detected.

When one or more parents or any close relatives of a baby are known to be carriers, or to have the disorder, a test will often be done shortly after birth. Parents can then be well prepared to spot any problems that may start from about six months onwards. They will also be able to take steps to prevent or minimize difficulties.

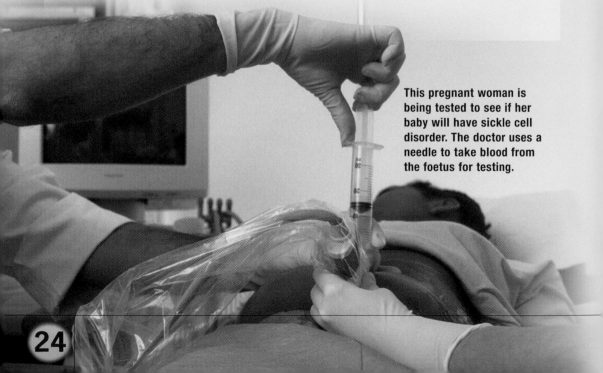

This pregnant woman is being tested to see if her baby will have sickle cell disorder. The doctor uses a needle to take blood from the foetus for testing.

In electrophoresis, different types of haemoglobin are identified in the laboratory by putting a small blood sample in an electric current.

Carriers

About one in ten Afro-Caribbeans and one in ten African Americans are carriers. In certain parts of Africa such as Nigeria, as many as one in five people are carriers. These people may be advised to have a test for sickle cell disorder before having an **anaesthetic**. This is because oxygen levels in the body sometimes become very low while under anaesthetic. This can cause blood cells to sickle. It is a sensible precaution but the risks of using anaesthetic for carriers of sickle cell disorder do not seem to be very different from the risks for other people.

Tests may also be done on a blood sample from a baby or cells taken from the placenta in the early stages of pregnancy. Parents may then face a difficult choice of whether or not to continue the pregnancy.

Being a carrier

Many hospitals test babies at birth to see if they have sickle cell disorder. But for every baby that is detected with the disorder as many as 100 **carriers** of the sickle cell **trait** may be found. These carriers have inherited only one copy of the sickle cell **gene**.

Carriers generally have excellent health. They live as long as other people and are no more likely to need hospital treatment during their life. However, in extreme conditions where there are low oxygen levels, such as on high mountains, in **unpressurized** aircraft and when scuba diving, there may be an additional risk.

Carriers may experience symptoms of sickle cell disorder when high up a mountain.

High altitudes

Occasional problems have been recorded in carriers travelling in unpressurized aircraft at altitudes above 3250 metres. These vary from relatively mild symptoms of a sickle cell **crisis** such as backache to a blocking of blood vessels in the **spleen**. Similar problems could occur when climbing in high mountains, particularly if a person remained at high altitude for a long time.

Passenger aircraft are now pressurized to an equivalent altitude of 1600–2300 metres. Problems have not been reported in carriers although people with sickle cell disorder occasionally have difficulties. Nevertheless, many commercial airlines exclude carriers from jobs as cabin crew.

Working for the armed forces

Sudden decompression can occur in military aircraft, exposing personnel to low air pressure. This risk has been considered by many armed services and employment policy towards carriers has varied. Carriers have in the past been excluded from working as pilots and co-pilots. Nowadays a test of the amount of sickle cell **haemoglobin** in a person's blood may be used to decide if an individual is suitable for the job.

A small risk of sudden death has been found in carriers during basic military training in the United States. In a study of 2 million recruits conducted by the Armed Forces Institute of Pathology it was found that carriers were 28 times more likely to experience sudden death compared with black recruits who were not carriers. However, the risk of death is still tiny compared with the total number of recruits who carry the sickle cell trait. Occasionally serious problems have been reported in civilians who are carriers following intense exercise.

Military aircraft may decompress rapidly, causing problems for carriers.

Who suffers from sickle cell disorder?

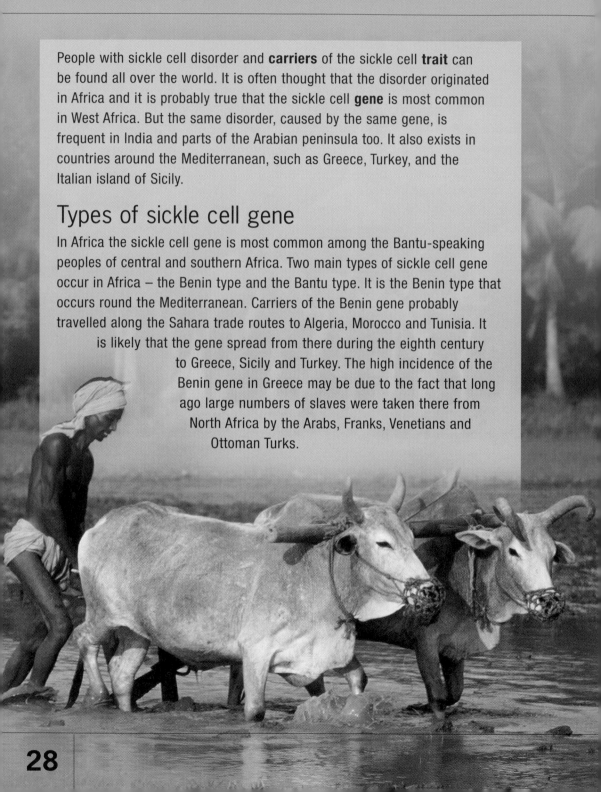

People with sickle cell disorder and **carriers** of the sickle cell **trait** can be found all over the world. It is often thought that the disorder originated in Africa and it is probably true that the sickle cell **gene** is most common in West Africa. But the same disorder, caused by the same gene, is frequent in India and parts of the Arabian peninsula too. It also exists in countries around the Mediterranean, such as Greece, Turkey, and the Italian island of Sicily.

Types of sickle cell gene

In Africa the sickle cell gene is most common among the Bantu-speaking peoples of central and southern Africa. Two main types of sickle cell gene occur in Africa – the Benin type and the Bantu type. It is the Benin type that occurs round the Mediterranean. Carriers of the Benin gene probably travelled along the Sahara trade routes to Algeria, Morocco and Tunisia. It is likely that the gene spread from there during the eighth century to Greece, Sicily and Turkey. The high incidence of the Benin gene in Greece may be due to the fact that long ago large numbers of slaves were taken there from North Africa by the Arabs, Franks, Venetians and Ottoman Turks.

The sickle cell gene is found all over the world and is particularly common in parts of India, such as Orissa, shown here.

The Benin gene

People with the same Benin gene were brought to North America by the slave trade between about 1650 and 1830. The sickle cell trait, usually the Benin type, now occurs in 8 per cent of African Americans in the United States and 10 per cent of Afro-Caribbeans. In Brazil 7 per cent of the black population carry the sickle cell trait. The gene is generally of the Bantu type because people taken as slaves to Brazil came mostly from Angola, Congo and Mozambique.

The sickle cell gene is very common in the huge population of central India, especially in Orissa, Maharastra and Madhya Pradesh. It is most common among certain tribal groups: the Chetty and Kurmar of Kerala, the Abhuj Maria of Madhya Pradesh and the Kondhs of Orissa. The gene found in India is different from the two African types.

Malaria – the killer

Sickle cell disorder is most common in the Tropics, in areas where **malaria** is most common. Malaria is caused by a **parasite** that is introduced into the body by a mosquito bite. The parasite enters the red blood cells of the person who has been infected, and then multiplies. The red cells burst and release the parasites, which then infect more red cells. The main symptoms are fever and weakness. Sometimes the parasite invades the brain, leading to coma and death unless prompt treatment is received.

This photograph, taken with a microscope, shows a section through red blood cells (coloured to show up) that have been infected with the malaria parasite.

Protective effects

People who are **carriers** of sickle cell disorder have greater resistance to malaria than people without the **gene**. The benefit has been found to be greatest in young children who have not yet acquired **immunity** to malaria and so are most vulnerable to it.

In Accra, Ghana, children of all ages who are carriers of sickle cell disorder have fewer malaria parasites in their blood than other children. In northern Ghana and Nigeria, where malaria is more severe and children gain immunity at an earlier age, the protective effect of being a carrier is limited to younger children under four years old. Older people and pregnant women in particular also seem to be protected by being carriers in areas where malaria is not so common and immunity is not so great.

Malaria kills a million people every year in Africa. Many more die from other diseases that they develop while weakened by malaria. In these extreme circumstances, resistance to malaria provided by the sickle cell gene gives people a distinct advantage. It enables them to survive when others die.

The advantage of being a carrier

Red blood cells from carriers are more delicate than normal red blood cells. Normally they do not sickle very much and so carriers have normal health, but they do tend to sickle when they are infected by the malaria parasite. These infected sickle cells are then more likely than normal cells to be filtered out by the **spleen** and recycled, killing the parasite.

This gives children who are carriers an extra resistance to malaria. They seem to survive better than children who are not carriers in areas that are infested with malaria mosquitoes. However, babies in rural Africa or India who inherit two copies of the sickle cell gene, and so suffer from the disorder itself, generally die during infancy. Despite these deaths the sickle cell gene remains present in large numbers of people in malarial areas because of the advantage it gives carriers.

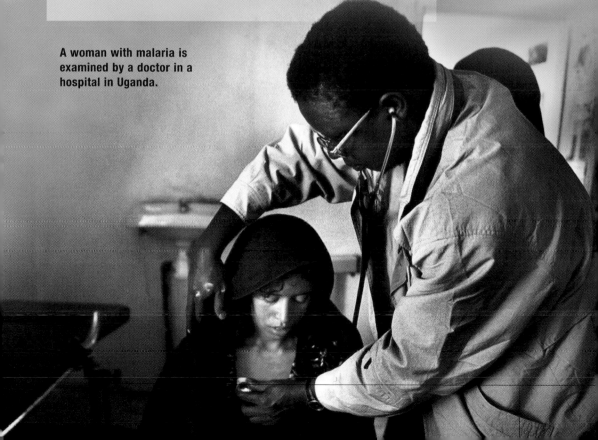

A woman with malaria is examined by a doctor in a hospital in Uganda.

Other sickle cell disorders

Haemoglobin C and beta-thalassaemia

There are over 200 different types of **haemoglobin** disorders that have some similarity to sickle cell disorder. The best known are haemoglobin C and **thalassaemia**. These conditions do not cause pain as in sickle cell disorder. Sometimes these other types of haemoglobin disorder occur together with the sickle cell **gene** and may then contribute to sickle cell disorder.

Haemoglobin C

Haemoglobin C or HbC is most common in Africa, particularly northern Ghana and Burkino Faso. In the Caribbean, between 2 and 5 per cent of people are **carriers** of the gene. People who inherit two copies of the HbC gene may have mild **anaemia** but they suffer few symptoms and develop normally in height and weight. However, HbC can cause serious illness in combination with sickle cell disorder.

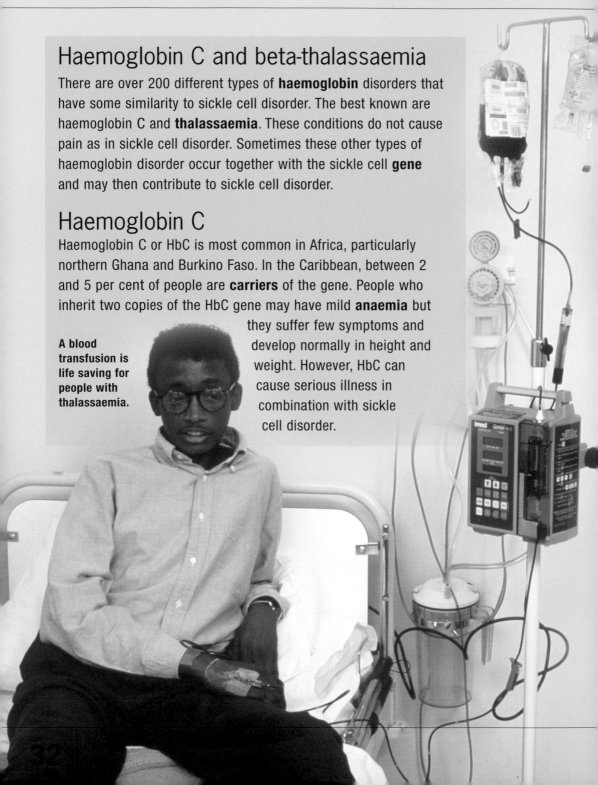

A blood transfusion is life saving for people with thalassaemia.

Thalassaemia

Thalassaemia is common in the Mediterranean and South-East Asia. It also occurs among African Americans and Afro-Caribbeans. The most serious form of the disease, thalassaemia major, causes haemolytic anaemia – a type of anaemia caused by destruction of red blood cells. People with this disorder suffer from fatigue and shortness of breath together with **jaundice** (yellowing of the whites of the eye) and enlargement of the **spleen**.

This child with thalassaemia is learning more about her condition.

Thalassaemia major is treated with blood **transfusions**, which are life saving. But after many transfusions the body becomes overloaded with iron, which comes from damaged red blood cells that have been recycled. This may bring on serious illnesses such as diabetes or heart failure.

Thalassaemia major and minor

Thalassaemia is an inherited disorder that reduces the normal production of **globin**. Globin is an essential part of haemoglobin, the red substance in blood. If a person inherits one gene for the disorder they are said to have thalassaemia minor, or thalassaemia **trait**. They are carriers of the disorder and it is not severe. If they inherit two genes for the disorder they are said to have thalassaemia major.

The evolving haemoglobin gene

For thousands of years humans have struggled to survive in areas of Africa infected with **malaria**. Over time the haemoglobin gene has evolved – gradually changed – to provide people with better protection against malaria. This is one of the best-known examples of human evolution.

The Dogon people

The Dogon people in Mali, West Africa, have a relatively high incidence of haemoglobin C and it protects them against severe malaria. Dogon people who have the haemoglobin C (HbC) gene seldom suffer from cerebral malaria – a very serious form of the disease in which the **parasite** invades the brain. The sickle cell gene is, on the other hand, relatively rare among the Dogon people. The sickle cell gene would probably be of little advantage to them when they already have the haemoglobin C gene.

Over the centuries African people have migrated within their continent and to other countries. As people mix and intermarry, various different combinations of haemoglobin genes occur.

Dogon people, shown here enjoying a celebration, often inherit a gene that prevents malaria from attacking the brain.

Sickle cell haemoglobin C

Sometimes the HbC gene occurs in the same person together with a single HbS (sickle cell) gene. That person may suffer from sickle cell disorder just as if he or she had two copies of the HbS gene. These people are said to have sickle cell-haemoglobin C disorder. They suffer from the same range of illnesses as in sickle cell disorder but in a much milder form. Their growth is not usually delayed or restricted and they generally seem to live as long as anyone else.

Thalassaemia gene combinations

There are also several different thalassaemia genes that can combine with the sickle cell gene. In Ghana about one person in 800 inherits the sickle cell-beta-thalassaemia combination of genes. In North America about one in 5000 African Americans are born with sickle cell thalassaemia. In Jamaica 1 in 23 babies born with sickle cell disorder have the sickle cell-thalassaemia combination.

In Greece, where thalassaemia is much more common, about half of the people with sickle cell disorder have the combined form. The severity of the disorder varies depending on the sickle cell gene combinations inherited and other factors.

Foetal haemoglobin

In the **foetus** and new-born baby, a special form of haemoglobin occurs called foetal haemoglobin. Generally it disappears during the first few months of life and is replaced by normal haemoglobin. However, some people have a gene that allows the foetal haemoglobin to persist in adult life. When this gene is inherited by itself there are no problems, but when it is inherited together with the sickle cell gene a person may suffer from mild sickle cell disorder.

Living with sickle cell disorder

T-Boz's story

'I have learnt to fake and smile when I wasn't happy, to sing when I didn't feel like it and to do things just to please my fans', says Tionne 'T-Boz' Watkins, member of the R&B band TLC from Atlanta, Georgia in the USA.

Now national celebrity spokesperson for the Sickle Cell Disease Association of America, T-Boz is explaining to the world how the disorder has affected her life. She says: 'Recently I have learned there was a larger stage than I could ever imagine, a stage that would enable me to take my message to those who needed it most.'

ⓕⓕOne thing I am trying to teach kids that nobody ever taught me is that nobody's flawless. If somebody says to me that I have bags under my eyes, that I look tired, well, honey, I am tired.ⓙⓙ

(Tionne 'T-Boz' Watkins, Sickle Cell Disease Association of America)

Childhood and teenage years

T-Boz suffered from recurring painful episodes of the illness as a child but did not know what it was until she was eight years old and the disorder was diagnosed. 'My attitude was…OK you're just going to have to face what you've got. Now suck it up and make the best of it,' T-Boz told *USA Today* reporter W. Reed Morgan.

During her teen years in Atlanta, T-Boz says: 'I was known as a sicko who couldn't do what normal kids were doing. I couldn't go swimming because the water was too cold, I had to drink special baby milk for my bones. I felt ugly.' About other teenagers with sickle cell disorder she says, 'There are teenagers who don't understand why they need more time to do things that normal teenagers do. There are children who may not have known until late in life about the "whys" of their pain.'

Climbing the mountain

Her illness did not stop T-Boz from reaching the top of her profession. In 1996 TLC won two Grammy awards (prestigious awards honouring great artistic achievement). In 2000 she was named by *People* magazine as one of the 50 most beautiful people in the world. But T-Boz has never even felt pretty. Her experience of what it is like to feel bad about herself and her ill health led her to write the song 'Unpretty'. T-Boz says she has 'climbed the mountain' herself and understands what others with sickle cell disorder have to endure. She knows what it is like to go straight from hospital to the recording studio so as not to let others down.

Now T-Boz is married to rapper Mack 10 and has a daughter, Chase Rolison, born in October 2000.

T-Boz (right) with fellow TLC band-member Chilli in 2002.

Living with sickle cell disorder

Julia's story

Julia Aruya was born in Lagos, Nigeria. She was the only one out of four children with sickle cell disorder and her parents were told by friends to let her die. 'My parents were encouraged to let me die because I was not a perfect child, a bad apple you might say,' says Julia.

Her father and mother took it in turns to take time off work to look after her and then took her to the United States for medical treatment. Julia graduated from college in Dallas, Texas, and obtained a job with a fashion retailer there.

A lack of tolerance

'I worked hard so as to avoid any extra workload for co-workers in case of absence. But due to my illness and pain **crises** I was absent from work for 30 to 90 days in a year. If you are not at work with minimal absence you are not promotable,' says Julia.

So she started a business at home, which turned out to be very successful. As a result she was offered a regular job again – this time in a multimillion dollar company with divisions all over the world. 'But I found the employers lacked tolerance for someone with sickle cell disability,' says Julia. 'After a year of mental anguish I decided to find another position.'

Like mother like daughter

Julia returned to running her own business and also works in higher education. Her colleagues understand her problems. But now she is going through similar difficulties with her daughter, Catherina, who also has sickle cell disorder.

'Her teacher actually said to me the other day: "Catherina is such a smart child. If only she would stop lying about her stomach and her back hurting all the time. She is always in pain, always sick, always going to the nurse and this is disruptive to the class." I went home and cried. Like me, my daughter has to fight so many battles.'

'My daughter's favourite thing is ice skating. She loves horseback riding and swimming. The sky is the limit, no limitations at all. I encourage her to do and be all she can be. She wants to be a medical doctor who finds a cure for sickle cell. I pray she does.' Julia wants to tell everyone with sickle cell to realize his or her potential.

Sickle cell crises can make it difficult to hold down a regular job.

The sickle cell crisis

People with sickle cell disorder can often tell when a **crisis** is coming on because their eyes begin to turn yellow (**jaundice**), they become thirsty or they are more tired or irritable than usual. But there are no clear signs to show that a person is experiencing pain. Some people may suffer without saying anything about it. Children must be trusted when they say they are in pain.

The frequency and severity of crises may be reduced by practical measures. People with sickle cell disorder are often advised to:
• drink plenty of water and other fluids to avoid **dehydration**
• avoid sudden changes of temperature by always wearing plenty of warm, dry clothing
• avoid strenuous sports in cold, wet weather
• avoid swimming unless the water is warm and care is taken not to get chilled while dressing.

It is important for people with the disorder to rest when they feel tired. Becoming overtired can cause a crisis. This is difficult for children to learn because they want to keep up with their friends.

People with sickle cell disorder should eat wisely and drink plenty of water.

Infections

Crises are often triggered by infections. People who have sickle cell disorder should be fully immunized against common diseases such as measles. Children may be advised to take penicillin every day to avoid chest infections, which may either trigger a crisis or follow on from one. They are often advised to take supplements of a vitamin, **folic acid**, which is found in fresh vegetables and fruit. Folic acid helps the body to replace blood that is lost during the breakdown of sickle cells.

How to cope with a sickle cell crisis

A sickle cell crisis may occur quite suddenly. The person becomes unwell and has severe pains in the abdomen and chest, stiffness of the neck or drowsiness. An individual having a sickle cell crisis generally needs urgent medical attention and may be best cared for in hospital. Powerful pain-relieving drugs can be given there.

If the crisis is not too severe, pain may be relieved at home with painkillers that can be bought over the counter in a chemist or shop. Deep breathing exercises, or other methods of relaxation, can also help to relieve pain. Gentle massage of the painful areas may also help.

Complications

Hospital treatment is needed when pain cannot be controlled with drugs that are available for use at home. Some painkilling drugs are restricted to use in hospital because they are very powerful, or because they have to be given by a drip into a vein. Other complications, such as a severe chest infection, may require intensive hospital care and the injection of **antibiotic** drugs.

Anaemia

Anaemia – a shortage of **haemoglobin** in the blood – deprives the body of oxygen. If there is a chest infection, a common complication, this further reduces the amount of oxygen in the blood **circulation**. Shortage of oxygen is likely to be particularly severe in painful areas that have become swollen. In these areas, small blood vessels are blocked by sickle cells, so normal red blood cells cannot get through to supply oxygen. In hospital, oxygen gas may be given to help the situation.

A person with a severe sickle cell **crisis** with worsening anaemia and other symptoms such as **pneumonia** may need an emergency blood **transfusion**. Usually this will be an exchange transfusion – blood from the patient is replaced with fresh blood. This removes some of the damaged blood cells and so reduces the work the body needs to do to remove them from the circulation. Patients may also receive regular blood transfusions to suppress production of sickle cell haemoglobin.

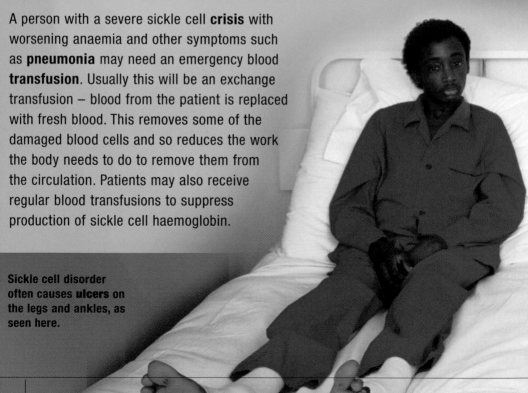

Sickle cell disorder often causes ulcers on the legs and ankles, as seen here.

Priapism

Another complication is **priapism** – unwanted and painful erection of the penis. This should be treated in hospital. If left untreated there is a danger of lasting damage, preventing normal erection.

Bed rest

Painful bones and joints may become deformed if they continue to bear weight. So patients may be advised to rest in bed or to wear a cast to stop them from moving a limb until the **inflammation** goes down. Patients may be transferred home for bed rest once they are stable.

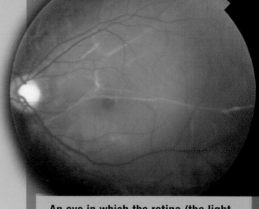

An eye in which the retina (the light-sensitive part) has become detached. The yellow lines are tears showing where the retina has been torn away. A detached retina can be repaired.

Complications requiring hospital treatment

- pain that can't be controlled at home
- swollen painful joints
- chest problems or pneumonia
- interruption of blood supply to the bowel
- severe swelling of the **spleen** or liver
- inflammation of the gallbladder
- kidney pain or blood in urine
- unwanted erection of the penis
- blood inside the eye
- detachment of retina
- severe headache or convulsions
- signs of a **stroke**, e.g. dizziness, confusion or slurred speech

New treatments

New drugs bring hope

Progress in clinical science and techniques in the last ten years have brought greatly improved treatment for patients with sickle cell disorder. Infections, brain injury, kidney disease, pain and **priapism** can all be prevented most of the time.

Hydroxyurea

One of the most effective ways of reducing the sickling of cells is to increase the amount of foetal **haemoglobin** in the **circulation**. Foetal haemoglobin is produced in the **foetus** and in babies. Normally very little is produced after the age of six months or a year but production of foetal haemoglobin can be stimulated with drugs.

Hydroxyurea is a drug prescribed in the USA for people who have frequent **crises** with the beginnings of damage to organs. It increases the production of foetal haemoglobin by acting on the cells that make haemoglobin. Hydroxyurea has been found to halve pain episodes, lung problems and admission to hospital in about 60 per cent of patients with these problems. However, in 2003, hydroxyurea was still on trial in the UK.

Nitric oxide

For patients who do not respond to hydroxyurea a number of other drugs are being produced. A particularly promising new approach is being developed in experiments with mice. A gas, nitric oxide, has been found to prevent the **dehydration** of cells and the formation of sickle haemoglobin into rods. Nitric oxide also makes it more difficult for sickle cells to pile up and block small vessels. Nitric oxide can be given as a drug, arginine, which makes the gas in the body.

Blood transfusions

Better ways are also being found to give blood **transfusions**, which are given when **anaemia** becomes very severe. Overload of the patient's body with iron (see page 33) can be avoided by using a process called **apheresis**. This removes damaged red cells from the circulation. When frequent blood transfusions are given, patients often begin to react to donated blood. Suitable donors become more difficult to find. Now that this is understood, blood can be matched more carefully and these difficulties can be avoided.

Together, these new approaches to treatment and new drugs provide substantial overall improvements for some patients. However, people with sickle cell disorder still spend their whole lives in and out of hospital, and on and off drugs such as painkillers and **antibiotics**.

A drug pump used in the treatment of sickle cell anaemia, with the catheter visible under the skin. It pumps a drug into a vein above the heart, which makes body iron dissolve so it can pass out of the body.

New treatments

Bone marrow transplantation

Treatment by transplantation of bone marrow, the body tissue that produces red blood cells, offers the possibility of a cure for sickle cell disorder. If normal bone marrow can be made to grow in someone with sickle cell disease then it will produce normal red blood cells that will replace the sickle cells. But this procedure can be done only when a suitable donor is available.

The treatment involves considerable risk because the bone marrow of the person with the disorder must first be destroyed by radiation. Until the bone marrow transplant has multiplied and reached sufficient size, a process that may take a few weeks, the patient lacks resistance to infection. He or she can easily die from a minor **virus** infection.

Because of the risk, bone marrow transplants are generally only considered for people who suffer more extreme forms of the disorder. These include those who have suffered a **stroke**, because there is a high risk of it happening again with severe or fatal results. Serious chest symptoms, which have a high risk of fatal complications, are another reason. People with frequent painful crises are considered too. The procedure is generally only offered to patients under 16 years of age in the UK and under 24 years in the USA. Younger patients are healthier and better able to survive the procedure.

Finding a donor

In order to transplant bone marrow, a suitable donor with matching body tissues, usually a relative, must first be found. Donors who are not related to the patient are now being used as well in some hospitals, enabling more people to benefit. But donors must have body tissues that closely match those of the patient. Experience in the United States has shown that a donor can be found for only about one in five patients.

The success rate

The transplant procedure is successful in over 80 per cent of patients. Painful crises no longer occur, their lungs work better and damage to their bones is halted. A normal life becomes possible for them.

However, about 7 per cent of patients who undergo the procedure die. Sometimes the grafted cells die and the patient is left without any working bone marrow. Sometimes the transplanted cells turn against the patient and attack body tissues with fatal results. And sometimes the radiation causes other complications.

Another 10 per cent of patients for whom the transplant is not successful survive the procedure. However, their treatment may not be a complete failure. Some patients have found that the condition is milder even though their transplant is not working properly.

Steady improvement in results can be expected in years to come as understanding of the difficulties increases. At present, bone marrow transplantation represents the best hope of a complete cure.

During a bone marrow transplant, bone marrow from a carefully matched donor is injected into the circulation.

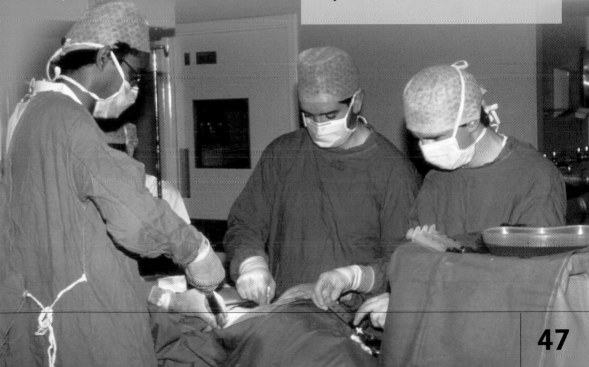

New treatments

Gene therapy

If the **gene** for normal haemoglobin could be inserted into the cells of people with sickle cell disorder, then the condition might be cured. That is the aim of gene therapy. Work began on gene therapy in 1979 and some 20 years later scientists began to get positive results. The first experimental treatments in human beings may begin in 2005.

Human genes into mice

Philippe Leboulch is a scientist working at the Massachusetts Institute of Technology and Harvard University, in the USA. After working on the problem for 10 years, Leboulch succeeded in transferring human genes into mice that had been transplanted with human cells producing sickle cell haemoglobin. The technique involves transferring genes by attaching them to a virus. The virus is then used to infect the bone marrow of the mice. The bone marrow is targeted because that is where the body makes red blood cells.

Successful gene therapy

The first successful results were obtained by Michel Sadelain at the Memorial Sloan-Kettering Cancer Center in New York, USA. Sadelain used gene therapy to correct **thalassaemia** in mice. A year after the correction was made, the mice were still producing normal haemoglobin. In 2001 Leboulch was able to correct sickle cell disorder in mice using an anti-sickling gene. The mice remained well, with improved production of haemoglobin a year later.

A long way to go

However, big problems remain before the therapy can be made suitable for people. The virus used to carry the gene into the mice was a form of HIV, the virus that causes AIDS. There is a question whether this might have bad effects on people in the long term. Better ways are also needed of removing unhealthy cells from bone marrow before fresh cells carrying the new gene can be inserted. Many more safety tests are needed before treatment of people can begin.

Human genes have been transferred to this mouse – carried into its body by a virus.

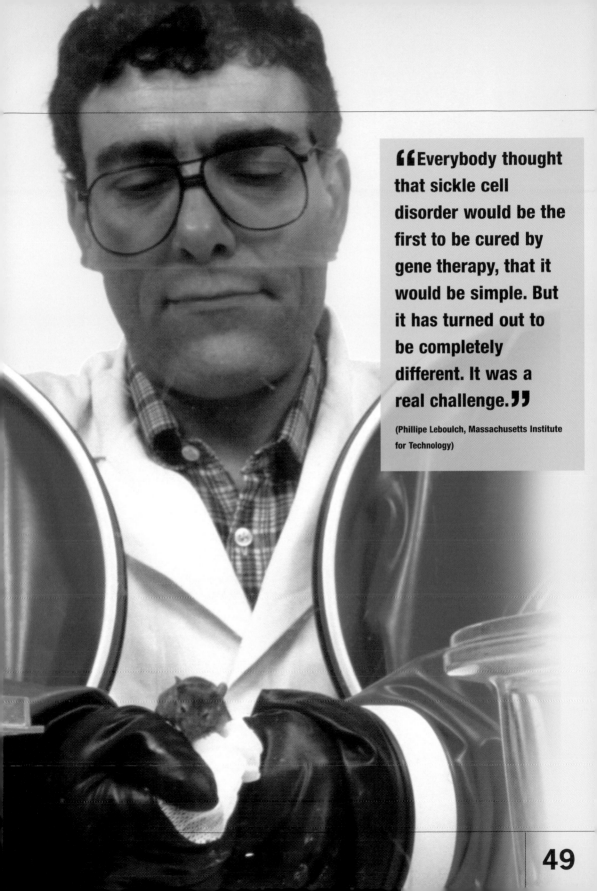

"Everybody thought that sickle cell disorder would be the first to be cured by gene therapy, that it would be simple. But it has turned out to be completely different. It was a real challenge."

(Phillipe Leboulch, Massachusetts Institute for Technology)

Hopes for a cure

Nowadays, with modern drugs and better understanding of the disease, many people with sickle cell disorder can live into their 50s and 60s. The pain that generally accompanies the disease is still difficult to control. But a deeper understanding of the disease has provided better guidelines for management.

Research

Research into sickle cell disorder has been intensive. It has provided the best-known example of human evolution in action – the struggle of the human body to fight the **malaria parasite**. But research in the lab has been slower to produce benefits for people who have the disorder.

Some people have argued that progress in producing new treatments for sickle cell disorder would have been faster if as many white people suffered from the condition. This may well be true. Yet progress has also been slow in finding remedies for other inherited diseases.

Only in very recent years have hopes of a cure been raised. Bone marrow transplants may now bring a complete cure for a few people. **Gene** therapy (see pp. 48–9) could also provide a cure for some people. If this is achieved in the next decade it will be a great triumph of science and medicine. Yet there are still important practical problems to be solved. The shortage of suitable donors and the cost is likely to restrict such treatments to a minority of people in Europe and North America.

More understanding

In rural Africa and India it will almost certainly continue to be a miracle if babies with sickle cell disorder survive beyond childhood. For most people with the disorder, including those in Europe and North America, substantial benefits may come from better application of the knowledge we already have. Increased understanding of new drugs and when they are best used, and early recognition of the disorder, will also bring benefits for many people.

Today, young people who have sickle-cell disorder will commonly live into their 60s. The future will hopefully bring new and even better treatments that improve the quality of life for people with the disorder.

Patient groups, which are increasingly influential, campaign to make sure that the best management methods are applied to patients in all social groups. They educate doctors and the public to help them to understand how best to help people with sickle cell disorder today, not just in the future.

Four children with sickle cell disorder

'Both of my parents are **carriers**,' says Santina Green, who was raised in Columbus, Ohio, 'and I am the oldest of four children, three girls and a boy, who all have sickle cell disease.'

'My parents had the hardest times looking after four children with the disease and trying to work as well. We were all patients at the Columbus Children's Hospital where we have been with **pneumonia** and had several blood **transfusions**. I would like to applaud both my parents for making sure we all got through school without being held back or having bad grades.

'Now my sisters and I all have children and they are all carriers. I thank God for that everyday.'

Information and advice

Patient groups are a most important source of help for people of all ages with sickle cell disorder, their relatives and friends. At these groups they can share information, discuss problems and find new solutions. They pool their resources, get experts to come and talk, and most important of all provide understanding for each other. They also provide information in leaflets and on websites, which ranges from details about other people's experiences and advice on day-to-day care through to high-level technical information.

Contacts in the UK

Sickle Cell Society
54 Station Road
London, NW10 4UA
Tel: 020 8961 7795
Website: www.sicklecellsociety.org
Website for children: www.sicklecellsociety.org/sicklescene/welcome.htm
The Sickle Cell Society provides information, support and contacts for people with sickle cell disorder in the UK.

Contacts in the USA

The Sickle Cell Information Center
PO Box 109, Grady Memorial Hospital
80 Jessie Hill Jr Drive SE, Atlanta,
Georgia 30303
Website: www.scinfo.org/
The Sickle Cell Information Center can provide information and a list of contacts including educational materials.

Sickle Cell Disease Association of America, Inc.
200 Corporate Pointe, Suite 495
Culver City, California 90230-8727
Website: www.sicklecelldisease.org/
The longest-running sickle cell research, education, and social services organization in the USA. On this site you can meet the Association's spokesperson, Tionne 'T-Boz' Watkins.

Contacts in Australia

Australian Thalassaemia Association
Website: wwwthal.murdoch.edu.au
The Australian Thalassaemia Association is an umbrella organization of societies working in the field of thalassaemia and related disorders.

Websites

Have A Heart For Sickle Cell Anemia Foundation

http://4sicklecellanemia.org
The website of a not-for-profit organization, the purpose of which is to improve the quality of life of those affected by sickle cell disease.

Fight Sickle Cell Disease

www.fightscd.com
A website dedicated to the fight against sickle cell disorder.

Dolan DNA Learning Center

www.yourgenesyourhealth.org
A multimedia guide to genetic disorders, including sickle cell disorder and beta-thalassaemia.

Disclaimer

All the Internet addresses (URLs) given in this book were valid at the time of going to press. However, due to the dynamic nature of the Internet, some addresses may have changed, or sites may have changed or ceased to exist since publication. While the author and Publisher regret any inconvenience this may cause readers, no responsibility for any such changes can be accepted by either the author or the Publisher.

Further reading

Sickle Cell Anaemia (Diseases and People), by Alvin Silverstein; Enslow Publishers, 1997. Explains the disease and uses stories of real people. Aimed at 9 to 12 year olds.

Sickle Cell Disease (Health Watch), by Susan Dudley Gold; Enslow Publishers, 2001. Follows the case of one child with the disorder and tells how he was cured by a stem cell transplant. Reading age 9 to 12.

Understanding Sickle Cell Disease, by Miriam Bloom; Roundhouse Publishing, 1995. Explains how sickle cell anaemia is inherited, describes its symptoms and treatment, and discusses the search for a cure.

Hope and Destiny: A Patient's and Parent's Guide to Sickle Cell Anemia, by Alan Sacerdote and Allen Platt; Independent Publishers Group, 2003. Personal discussion of the disorder and guide to medically proven treatment written for African Americans. Contains advice on suffering and life issues.

Glossary

amino acids
substances that combine in long chains to form proteins

anaemia
a medical condition in which someone has too little haemoglobin in their blood cells

anaesthetic
a drug that makes a person unable to feel anything, especially pain, in the whole body or part of the body

antibiotic
a drug that kills bacteria or prevents their growth, and can cure infections

apheresis
a process that separates cells in the blood and returns the good cells to the body

bacteria
the smallest and simplest forms of life, which are often a cause of disease

carriers
people who have inherited one copy of the haemoglobin S gene; they do not have sickle cell disorder but could pass it on to their children

circulation
blood circulates round the body – the heart, arteries and veins together are known as the circulation

crisis
the name given to an attack of sickle cell disorder

dactylitis
inflammation and swelling of the fingers

dehydration
the loss of water from the body

discrimination
treating a group of people worse than other groups

fertile
in men: able to make a woman pregnant; in women: able to get pregnant

foetus
a baby in the early stages of pregnancy

folic acid
a vitamin found in fresh green vegetables that is essential for normal growth and multiplication of cells

gene
unit inside a cell that controls a particular aspect of a living thing that has been passed on from its parents

genetics
the scientific study of the ways in which different features are passed down from parents to children

globin
four globin molecules join together with a haem molecule to make a haemoglobin molecule

haem
one haem molecule joins together with four globin molecules to make haemoglobin

haemoglobin
the red substance in blood – made up of one haem molecule and four globin molecules

hormone
a chemical substance, such as the male hormone testosterone, which is released into the body in one place and has an effect in another place

immunity
the body's ability to avoid infection and fight off disease

inflammation
a condition in which a part of the body becomes red, sore and swollen because of infection or injury

jaundice
a condition in which the whites of the eyes and the skin become yellow because the body cannot dispose of a yellow-brown substance, bilirubin, which accumulates in the blood

malaria
a serious disease, caused by a parasite in the blood, which can be fatal

molecules
the smallest units of a chemical

parasite
a creature that lives in or on another creature

pneumonia
inflammation of the lungs caused by infection

prejudice
negative feelings towards a group of people that are not based on factual information

priapism
unwanted painful erection of the penis

protein
large molecules made up of hundreds or thousands of amino acids linked in chains

seizures
brief spells when the messages inside the brain get mixed up and the person loses control of his or her body

septicaemia
poisoning of the blood caused by infection

spleen
an organ that removes worn-out blood cells from the circulation and fights infection

stroke
a sudden serious illness when a blood vessel in the brain bursts or is blocked

testosterone
male sex hormone that is produced by the testes

thalassaemia
an inherited blood disorder in which haemoglobin is not produced in the normal quantity

tissues
mass of cells that form the different parts of humans, animals and plants

trait
a condition that is inherited

transfusion
transfer of blood into a person's body to replace blood lost in an accident or to correct anaemia

ulcers
open sores on the skin

unpressurized
in an aircraft, when the air pressure is not kept the same as it is on Earth; in a pressurized aircraft, the air pressure is kept the same

virus
the smallest known living thing that causes infectious disease

Index

Titles in the *Need to Know* series include:

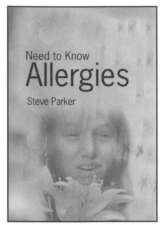

Need to Know
Allergies
Steve Parker

Hardback   0 431 09760 7

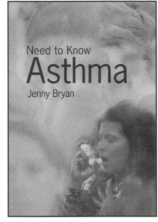

Need to Know
Asthma
Jenny Bryan

Hardback   0 431 09761 5

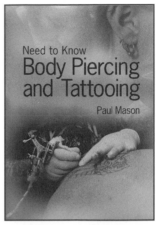

Need to Know
Body Piercing and Tattooing
Paul Mason

Hardback   0 431 09818 2

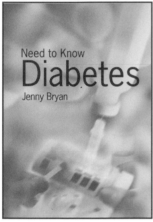

Need to Know
Diabetes
Jenny Bryan

Hardback   0 431 09762 3

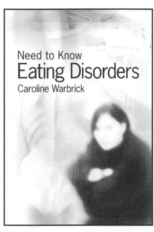

Need to Know
Eating Disorders
Caroline Warbrick

Hardback   0 431 09799 2

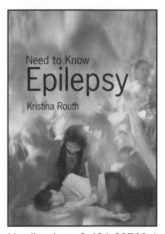

Need to Know
Epilepsy
Kristina Routh

Hardback   0 431 09763·1

Need to Know
Multiple Sclerosis
Alexander Burnfield

Hardback   0 431 09764 X

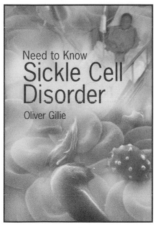

Need to Know
Sickle Cell Disorder
Oliver Gillie

Hardback   0 431 09765 8

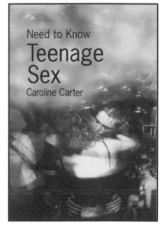

Need to Know
Teenage Sex
Caroline Carter

Hardback   0 431 09821 2

Find out about the other titles in this series on our website www.heinemann.co.uk/library